Me Not Me

Me Not Me

Become Who You Want To Be
By Recovering From Your Past

Kayt Campbell

Contents

Preface

"Security is mostly a superstition. It does not exist in nature, nor do the children of men as a whole experience it. Avoiding danger is no safer in the long run than outright exposure. Life is a daring adventure or nothing at all."
~ Helen Keller, famous American author, political activist and lecturer, first deaf blind person to earn a Bachelor of Arts degree.
1810-1968

If you are reading this book, hopefully it is because you are interested in finding a clear and straight forward way to make some discernable changes in your life, and with any luck those changes would be for the better—that's exactly what I was doing back in the seventies when I started exploring self help paradigms.

My life at the time wasn't as bad as some, but clearly fell short of what I had expected it to be during my idealistic musings as a teenager. I just knew life could be better than mine was and I was determined to find out how to make it so. This determination launched my life in a new direction and towards outcomes that I could never have predicted. This pursuit ultimately became my life's work.

In all my years of studying, traveling, and teaching I don't recall meeting anyone who does not desire to experience life with more ease, more pleasure, or less of the undesirable stuff. Virtually everyone I've ever met has some area of their lives they would like to improve. My personal mission statement was born out my motivation to improve my life and my desire to work with like-minded souls. I decided early in my career as a personal development coach, that my purpose was to "work with people like me who wish to improve the quality of their lives" which became, and still is, my mission statement.

There is a vast selection of helpful organizations and therapists available for people with clinical diagnoses, but for us folks just doing our best to get from one end of our lives to the other—not so much. For those of us surviving our lives in quiet desperation, I felt we deserved to have a better shot at a happy life. I was determined to find out how to do that and to share what I discovered with anyone interested in hearing about it.

I set out to find a way to have a happy life and that's the kind of support I wanted to be for others in their pursuits. Down through the years I've added every bit of experience, both mine and my clients, to the bank of knowledge I use to guide us to our goals. Nearly forty years of distilling that bank of knowledge into a simple, quick to learn, and easy to apply technology resulted in the Me, not Me Process.

This book explores attention and experience, the relationships of attention and experience to each other, and how to use attention to change experience. It is ultimately about how to remember who we really are, to differentiate that from what we are not, and to live a life that shows it.

What if we had the ability to experience our lives with grace and happiness?

What if we had the ability to experience our lives from that calm center of our beings that is who we really are? I hope you find some of your own answers here.

1

Create A Life of Grace and Happiness

"Inherently, each one of us has the substance within,
to achieve whatever our goals and dreams define.
What is missing from each of us is the training,
education, knowledge and insight to utilize what
we already have."

Author Mark Twain, aka Samuel Langhorn Clemens, 1839-1910, a beloved American author of 28 books, numerous short stories, and sketches.

At the time I began my search for ways to improve my lot in life I had a long list of health problems, most of which were associated with stress. I was in a marriage that was seriously not working for me, I was putting in very long hours seven days a week and there seemed to be no end to the ever increasing demands being made on my time and energy. If that wasn't enough I was attempting to raise four children, manage a huge household and handle my husband's business. There was simply no time or space for any of my needs to be met. At the time, I was so busy I didn't realize I had needs, much less that they weren't being met. I had a medicine cabinet full of prescriptions growing every month. One day a chiropractor suggested that if I didn't do something, and soon, I was going to break.

The medical profession was not making matters any better. The doctors simply gave me more and more drugs in the attempt to mask a growing list of symptoms. I came from a background of believers in vitamins and nutrition therapy, so I even tried changing my diet.

That approach was a little like trying to wash an elephant with a toothbrush. The problem was quite a bit bigger than the simple solution of improving the quality of my nutrition. If I was going to fix my life, I was going to have to use a broader brush.

Mind Control

I had been plagued with premonitions, prophetic dreams and psychic experiences since I was a child and I decided to start there. Maybe if I could get that piece figured out I would be able to sort out some of the other stresses in my life. The very first self awareness thing I did was a course that explored the inner working of our minds. What I got out of that course was the information that I was indeed psychic*, clairvoyant even. There was an explanation for the experiences I had been having for so long. I actually found comfort knowing I wasn't crazy, I was just psychic. Actually we were told everyone has some level of psychic ability. What a relief! I took my certificate from the completion of the training, put it in a book on the shelf, and carried on with my struggle.

*psychic--dictionary definition: outside the sphere of scientific knowledge. My use of the word psychic in this book refers to the idea that we are all connected to all that is through the phenomena of something more commonly accepted as intuition.

Dictionary definition of intuition: something known or believed instinctively, without actual evidence for it. I'm not visiting the parlor game with crystal balls and silk draped fortune tellers. Clairvoyance would simply be a very highly developed sense of intuition. I chose to use the word psychic because that is how it was presented to me in that course I took.

The mind control course brought me to my first learning experience and lasting realization. Throughout this book I will list these "learnings" approximately in the order in which they occurred to me.

Learning #1: We're all "psychic" to some extent. That information made it possible for me to seriously entertain the news bulletin "We are all one," expressed in later teachings.

While the psychic awareness course helped relieve my anxiety about perhaps having a screw loose, it didn't do much for the physical stuff I had going on or what I was going to do about the husband who was driving me up the wall.

Rebirthing

The next thing that sparked my interest was a thing called Rebirthing. I had been told this technique had helped many of its advocates with an impressive array of long standing physical maladies. I had to do something. The quantity of prescriptions I was taking was really getting out of hand. Off I went to study Rebirthing.

To my near disbelief and total delight the sessions I underwent with a dedicated and talented Rebirther* began to relieve my symptoms within a few weeks. I was assisted in identifying the memories connected with my physical symptoms and given instructions on how to change my thoughts, how to change my assumptions about my life, and thereby change what I was experiencing. Halleluiah! This was great stuff. Within a very short time my health improved so much I was through with the prescription medicines, I was yelling at the children a lot less and my husband was . . . well at least the other things were getting better. I was hooked. My family was just going to have to put up with my absence during the time I was spending on my new pursuits.

* A *Rebirther* is a person who is trained in facilitating sessions of a specific breathing technique designed to allow memories being held in the physical body to surface, be examined and addressed with a variety of affirmations and life changing decisions.

Learning #2: The experiences we have in life effect us physically. Our bodies hold memories of traumas and injuries and until these things are identified and dealt with they affect us. Getting in touch with those feelings and the assumptions they are connected with and changing those assumptions is a big step in the direction of healing, real physical healing.

From time to time, I will share stories to illustrate a point.

A Story about Mark

Eventually I decided to become certified as a Rebirther. I had so much improvement in my life from the sessions I wanted to learn how to share the method with others. Also the business of teaching things I've studied is a tendency that is a part of my personal pattern. Everything I have ever studied, that has had a positive impact on my life, I've gone on to master to the extent that I would have the ability to teach it. Not to mention that taking a skill to the next level also enhances my chances of making gains with it. I've never denied that I've always been in this to improve my life. If others want to pick up on what I've learned—great! This kind of goes back to that "we are all one" thing I referred to earlier.

Now, I've become a Rebirther and I have clients who are making positive gains. I've integrated the concepts and techniques to a level of expertise which enables me to be supportive of those who wish to make gains for themselves. Then one day a man presented to me with the most classic example of Learning #2 that I have seen to this day.

I'll call him Mark (not his name) for the purpose of this story.

Mark had a problem with a sore shoulder. He had been to the doctor and the X-rays showed nothing abnormal. In his work with a physical therapist he would feel some improvement but then the soreness would return. The pain in Mark's shoulder was sporadic in nature. It would come and go and show up at odd times without any apparent reason. He had actually come to me for Rebirthing sessions for other reasons, he just happened to mention the shoulder pain to me one day. I suggested that we focus attention on it during a session and he was willing.

There is an interesting thing about attention. Attention can get stuck on a thing, thought, person, event, place, etc., but then we can also deliberately focus attention on those things we want to put it on. Attention can seem to be a function of what external thing is grabbing our attention but we can also choose where to put our attention, if we so decide. Attention is much more of a two way street than perhaps we had assumed before.

During Mark's session I suggested he put attention on his shoulder while using the prescribed style of breathing for a rebirthing session. As he applied this breathing technique I encouraged him to focus more attention on the shoulder with each breath. Eventually the memory (muscle memory) surfaced. When he was a boy his father would punch him in the shoulder whenever he made a mistake. Mark had created an association of being wrong or making a mistake with the punches (and pain) in his shoulder. In his life whenever Mark felt that he was in error or making a mistake his shoulder would start hurting. No wonder his shoulder pain seemed so sporadic and unpredictable.

After that session I gave Mark the suggestion to change his thought from "I'm wrong" to "It's Okay to be wrong." He had very few episodes of shoulder pain after that, and on the few occasions that he did, he would reaffirm his new conclusion. Soon enough the shoulder pains ceased entirely, never to return.

This experience clearly illustrated the mind-body connection to me. I've never forgotten it.

Chapter One Main Points:

Take your life into your own hands. Study, explore, read, research, make yourself your own laboratory experiment. You are the only one with the ability to discover what there is to know about you. It will help you get to where you want to go with your life if you know what you have to work with. This project alone can be a lifetime pursuit and it is worth it.

Learning #1

We're all "psychic" to some extent. That information made it possible for me to seriously entertain the news bulletin "We are all one," expressed in later teachings.

Learning #2

The experiences we have in life effect us physically. Our bodies hold memories of traumas and injuries and until these things are identified and dealt with they affect us. Getting in touch with those feelings and the assumptions they are connected with and changing those assumptions is a big step in the direction of healing, real physical healing.

2

Your Journey

"Find out what you are passionate about and then live a life that shows it." Author unknown

I have continued, to this day, to study consciousness* work. This and the people I've had the pleasure to study and work with are sources of endless fascination for me. It has been through the pursuit of awareness that I have collected the lessons I will share in this book and led to the Me, not Me process I share with you at the end of this book.

*Consciousness work: learning to examine our thoughts and beliefs in order to determine the causes of the conditions of our lives. The study of how (and why) our conscious minds arrive at the states they are in and how to change those states if we so choose.

Me, not Me--Become Who You Want To Be By Recovering From Your Past

When I refer to "Me" I'm talking about the beings who are complete and perfect just as we came into this incarnation. This is the "Me" who is without the limitations of layers of beliefs/identities we have acquired by means of all the life experiences we have had. This encompasses a nearly infinite variety of influences including but not limited to all the indoctrinations we have been exposed to and the ideas and ideals of cultures and societies. I'm talking about the "Me" who is free of those influences or not at the effect of them. I'm referring to that calm, peaceful adept at the core of every one of our beings who is perfectly capable of creating a life of ease and pleasure. I'm talking about beings capable of creating a more ideal life without the burdens of unconsciously perpetuated behaviors that limit our ability to think and act in a deliberate fashion.

When I speak of the "not Me" I am referring to the experience of that same "Me" after layers of beliefs/identities have been adopted and misowned as who we are. We are not all—or any—of those things, we really are pure spirit here to have a human experience. Granted, human experience requires that we have some beliefs/identities in order to have it; however, we can consciously choose which of those identities to have our experiences through. Integrating those resisted experiences to clear the path to having the life we prefer is what my life and this book are all about.

Once learned and practiced, the Me Not Me process allows you to live a life that will be more a demonstration of you as a spiritual being and less of the unconsciously adopted limitations which created the resistances you've been experiencing. That's where Living the Difference Between Who You Are and What You're Not comes into play. It's a nice way to live.

I'm not about to tell you who you are and how things should work for you. I've written this to relate what I've learned over the last 40 plus years of exploring and studying personal empowerment work, how things work for me, and to offer these experiences and things I've learned for your examination and evaluation for their possible value to you. There is a little bit of everything I've ever been exposed to in these pages and in the Me, not Me process.

The technique itself is an easy to learn and simple to apply process—a compilation of core principles that have stood the test of time. Each step of the process utilizes one or more of those principles to form a sequence of steps taking the participant into an experience of integration, which frees them of limiting constructs affecting their lives.

Easy to Learn and Apply

Not only are the steps of the process easy to learn and apply, it is also portable. Once you've practiced it a few times it is yours to use whenever you feel the need or desire to do so and you won't need a practitioner or therapist to take you through it. At the end of this book I've listed some coaches who can be helpful in the application of the Me, not Me process to your life issues should you desire some guidance.

The process can be accomplished in just a few minutes and can be done anywhere you can be quietly focused for those few minutes. Of course, the privacy of your own home is ideal and it has been successfully applied while sitting on a park bench, in an airplane, or sitting alone in a coffee shop. Your choice of location depends upon your ability to direct your attention. This cognitive process requires focus so you would never attempt to do it while your attention is required for any other activity like driving a car. My suggestion is that you practice it at home until you feel comfortable with your skill level before attempting it in more public venues.

Before I delve into the steps of the process I'm going to discuss those core principles I referred to earlier. I think it helps to grasp a technique if we understand the origins of it.

Above all, enjoy your journey!

Chapter Two Main Points:

Find something that works for you, then master it. If you realize that the paradigm you are operating with has come to the end of its potential, find another one.

Study, research, self examination, and consciousness exploration are a way of life, not a destination that you ever arrive at. Self actualization is a journey.

The Me, not Me process I teach in this book is a way to move yourself into a relaxed and peaceful life and it never hurts to explore the other things available. I studied everything that I heard about. Some things turned out to be essentially useless, except perhaps for entertainment value and in others I found gold.

I wrote this book so you wouldn't have to sort through the milieu unless, of course, you find that interesting like I did.

Attention Where?

"It ain't what they call you, it's what you answer to."
Author W.C. Fields ~ American comedian, actor, juggler (known as The Great McGonigle), and writer. 1880-1946

Since the technique I'm about to share with you is based on the natures of attention and experience and their relationship to each other, I think it would be a good idea to discuss these concepts a bit before we move on to the process.

Let's talk about attention. Where does it come from, where does it go and how does all this happen?

Have you ever noticed how something that annoys you (e.g. a repetitive sound or movement) takes more and more of your attention? First you notice it, then you listen for it, wait for it, know that it is going to be there and then you can't wait for it to stop or you even try to make it stop! Your attention becomes so absorbed in it that everything else fades into the background or seems to cease to exist in your awareness entirely. You might even stop what you were doing before this noise or disturbance appeared and devote all of your attention to it. It *has* your attention.

It also works with enjoyable experiences, those moments when we enjoy the suspension of time and place and experience the moment. You might be cuddling your baby or losing yourself in a particularly lovely piece of music. Everything but what you have your attention on seems to disappear.

Imagine one of these experiences in your life and then notice what your experience of time was. Did you have any awareness of time? Did time seem to drag on or fly by? Our sense of time can be influenced by whether we are resisting or desiring what we are experiencing . . . more about this later.

Now that we are more aware of attention and how it can affect us, let's do an exercise to strengthen our control of our attention. This exercise can be very relaxing and can actually lead to that calm state talked about by those who meditate.

Attention Exercise 1: (Please consider reading all the way through the instructions for this exercise before doing it)

Step 1: Focus your attention on an object in your immediate environment. Study it closely. Continue to examine the object until you are absorbed in it, until it seems to be the only thing you are aware of. If your attention wanders just bring it back. Relax and enjoy the experience.

Step 2: Take your attention off the object and bring it back to yourself.

Step 3: Choose another object in your immediate environment study it intently, continue to intensify your attention on the object until you are absorbed in it, until it seems to be the only thing you are aware of. Relax and enjoy the experience.

Step 4: Repeat this sequence several times, placing attention on an object and then bringing your attention back to yourself, until you have done this 3 or 4 times.

Now answer these questions: As you were focusing on the last object did you have any attention left on the first object? Did you have a sense of time passing while you were focusing on the objects? If you answered yes to either of these questions repeat the exercise until you can relax into it and have the experience of everything fading away except what you are focusing on.

This "fading away of everything else" is an experience that I first had during long sessions of meditation. Eventually my skill strengthened and I was able to focus my attention so effectively that I could quickly quiet my mind and find a calm center within which to exist. Meditation became another tool in my arsenal of stress reducing techniques.

It will become effortless to focus your attention where you direct it. As that skill strengthens you will notice that when you have your attention placed on something everything else falls into the background, frequently to the extent that you have no awareness of them.

For instance, when you are intensely focused on something your awareness of outside noises could diminish to the extent of being non-existent for you. E.g. you wouldn't hear a motorcycle outside.

If you are bored, you can be easily distracted because your attention isn't being directed to anything in particular.

This next exercise will strengthen your skill with deliberately focusing your attention even more.

Attention Exercise 2: (Please consider reading all the way through the instructions for this exercise before doing it)

Step 1 - Consciously put your attention on something in the room and decide how long you will look at it. Set a timer if you have one. Decide how long you will look at something and set the timer for that duration. Examine it with all of your attention. Actually study it. Notice its size, shape, characteristics, color, weight, etc. If your attention wanders, bring it back to the object. When the timer stops bring your attention back to yourself. Notice if the time seemed longer or shorter than you had expected it to.

Step 2 - Now, very consciously shift your attention to another object and set the timer again. Continue repeating this sequence until you have done it three or four times.

The ability to deliberately put your attention on something, and decide how long you will hold your attention on that object will expand your awareness and build your skill with controlling your attention. As your skill level increases your self-awareness increases and puts you in the driver's seat of your experiences. This is an outcome of controlling the location of your attention.

Learning #3: We can amplify what we are experiencing by putting more attention on it and we can diminish the experience of something by reducing the amount of attention we have on it.

Learning #4: We can control the location of our attention.

"As long as you derive inner help and comfort from anything, keep it."
Mohandas K Gandhi ~1869-1948 often referred to as Mahatma meaning great soul. He pioneered the concept of resistance to tyranny through mass civil disobedience, a philosophy firmly founded upon nonviolence.

A Story about Fire Walking

In case you've ever wondered, as I did, how in the world someone could walk over a bed of hot coals without getting their feet badly burned, here's the answer.

I went to a seminar led by a famous teacher of advanced self-help technologies. At this seminar one of the outcomes we were told to expect was the ability to do a fire walk*. The fire walk would not be compulsory, but you would be prepared for it if you chose to do it. We were taken to the parking deck of the hotel where we were staying. There, a team of experienced fire builders was working feverishly to create a long bed of glowing coals for us to traverse.

*A fire walk is literally walking over a bed of glowing hot coals. It is an exercise in controlling your attention to the extent that your body is unaffected by the heat of the coals. You can actually control your attention to the extent that you can walk across 15 or 20 feet of smoldering red coals without sustaining any injury. Many people have spent (wasted) a lot of time trying to figure out what the trick is. There is no trick. If you don't learn to control your attention you get burned. I've been there, I've seen it.

We went back into the seminar room and spent the next two days in the singular activity of being trained to put the focus of our attention on what specifically we wanted it to be on. We were taught guided meditations. We were taken through attention exercises somewhat similar to the ones that I've shared with you. We were given all manner of instruction to prepare us for the fire walk experience.

At the end of the seminar, we were taken back to the parking lot where the bed of glowing coals lay waiting for us. The first ones to walk over the coals were the instructor and some of his team members. I think they went first just to show us that indeed it could be done. Then one of our group bravely stepped up and away he went! His success spurred on more students until the ranks of those left behind were thinning and that included me.

At some point I made the decision to go for it and without further deliberation I stepped up to the line, received my final pep talk and away I went, looking up at the sky, and saying the words over and over again "cool moss, cool moss." The visualization being that I was walking over a bed of cool moss

To say that this was an exhilarating experience is a glorious understatement. I was blasted into another level of awareness of the power of controlling my attention. It also brought home to me the real meaning of the expression "internal locus of control."* I got a lot out of it and I'm not recommending that anyone else do it--ever. I got the point and the point of this book is that I can share what I learned with you here and you don't have to go out and do what I did in order to get this information, unless you just want the hands on experiences for yourself.

*"Internal locus of control" is a phrase that refers to ones ability to place or direct their attention based solely upon a determination coming from within themselves. E.g. "She has a highly developed internal locus of control." This statement means she has the ability to direct, amplify or diminish the amount of attention she places, and determine the duration her attention is located in a specific place or on a specific object. The internal locus of control is a skill one develops with practice.

Learning #5: The ability to deliberately put my attention where I want it is enormously important, beneficial, and empowering. (Is it possible to practice those attention exercises enough?)

If we perceive attention as though it is a physical commodity and each of us has a finite supply of it, like a pile of sand, available to us for use we can get an idea of how valuable the deliberate direction and use of attention is. We can use those grains, or bits of attention, from that hypothetical "pile of sand" in any way we choose if it hasn't already been used up.

Free or Stuck Attention?

Free attention is attention that is not already being used for some purpose or is not "stuck" in such a way as to not be available for our deliberate use any longer.

Some examples of attention in use--and therefore not presently available for other things: While driving a car our attention is (hopefully) on the road and the action of navigating the roads and traffic. The danger of texting on a cell phone while driving has been demonstrated so many times it is now against the law to engage in it in many places. This is classic split attention or placing attention on more than one activity with the resulting attention deficit being so great as to endanger lives.

An example of "stuck" attention is attention that is buried in some past trauma to the extent that those attention particles cannot be resurrected for any other use. A past trauma like the loss of a loved one, a past event so frightening it still causes a limitation to our lives, or a situation that we are currently involved in so dangerous or emotionally charged we can't think of anything else. If a person is frightened by a dog as a child this may make it nearly impossible for that adult to be in the presence of any dog without experiencing paralyzing fear. This is a classic example of "stuck" attention.

Having free attention for deliberate use is incredibly empowering, and amazingly increases our ability to function. A symptom of a diminished supply of free attention is a notably limited ability to function in the world. A short attention span, poor memory—being easily distracted, being disorganized, having a chaotic life are all symptoms of depleted attention. An indicator of a large quantity of free attention is demonstrated by highly functional, well-organized, deliberate individuals who enjoy a peaceful and happy life.

One of the purposes of the Me, not Me process taught in this book is to free stuck attention to increase your supply of free attention giving you a heightened ability to function and be more deliberate in your life. The quantity of attention available for us to use can be increased and this process is an effective way to do that. A highly developed deliberate placement of attention also explains how someone can walk on hot coals without getting burned to a crisp.

Chapter Three Main Points:

It really is all about the deliberate use of attention. Mastering the placement of and the use of attention is the key to success in so much in life that without it we're pretty much wasting our time flailing around like sheets in the wind.

Learning #3: We can amplify what we are experiencing by putting more attention on it and we can diminish the experience of something by reducing the amount of attention we have on it.

Learning #4: We can control the location of our attention.

Learning #5: The ability to deliberately put my attention where I want it is enormously important, beneficial, and empowering. (Is it possible to practice those attention exercises enough?)

Experience What?

*"Do you want an adventure now or would you like
to have your tea first?"*
Peter Pan ~ A magical, free spirited character created by Scottish novelist
and playwright J. M. Barrie in 1902

How is it that we come to have an experience? What makes up an experience, what are the components of it, the mechanism of it?

Without getting into a long philosophical dissertation on this subject of experience I'm just going to share some of my personal observations about it with you.

The definition of an experience is an event in consciousness that makes up part of an individual life, something encountered, undergone or lived through. Fair enough, but how are those events perceived, where do they come from and what makes them possible? I actually think about stuff like this.

In order for me to *have* an experience I have to be separate from the thing being experienced. Think about it. If something is part of me like the color of my eyes, I don't have any attention on it because it is a part of me. I don't think about my eyes or what color they are, because they are part of me, I've integrated them. I don't look at them I see through them. Even in the mirror I have to consciously direct attention at my eyes in order to examine them; otherwise I'm simply looking through them.

I can't experience a strawberry's aroma, scent, taste, texture or visual aspects if I am the strawberry. I must be outside of it, different from it in order to have an experience of it. I must be able to observe something in order to be able to experience it. I'm here—it's there. I'm Me—it isn't Me. And there we have it folks. Something is either Me or it's not Me.

If something is not me I can have an experience of it. If something is integrated into the totality of me, if it is me, then I'm not experiencing it, I'm existing as it.

Separation or integration; that is the question. Or maybe it's the answer. We've been told that resistance is not a good thing, but a little resistance is necessary in order for us to be separate from anything. In that instance, resistance to something, which leads to separation from it allows us to have experiences. It can be a good thing--or not. We each get to decide what we prefer and after we've done that we can decide to either remain separate, thereby experiencing, or integrate, thereby ceasing to experience. It's a pretty simple recipe and it's the formula that has evolved out of many years of exploring, testing and proving. It's the Me-not Me formula.

The simplest form of resistance is to say "that's not Me." When we've accepted something into our consciousness (into our own personal universes) by declaring that it "is Me," then we have integrated it and no longer experience it as separate from us. We actually no longer have any experience of it.

A Story about a Guy I Love

At some point in this love story, there was an event that completely brought home to me the power of accepting an experience into my being, giving it a place in my universe, integrating it, and thereby ceasing to experience the event. I had been in deep grief for years and

I felt trapped in an unending cycle of resistance and despair—but I digress.

I met this amazing man and we fell crazy in love with each other. We had a whirlwind romance that lasted about 10 months. We were making all sorts of plans and we were excited about our new lives together. And then one day he died. I had been out on a trip and I received the news of his demise upon returning home. I was completely devastated. This event vectored my life to an amazing extent. In that moment, everything changed for me.

I spent the next 2 years processing the loss of him in every way I could. I used every tool I had ever learned. I sought the guidance of every friend who could bear to go there with me. I did it all. I moved to a place by the sea, the place where he and I had talked about creating our new lives together. After two years of attempting to work through my grief I decided to move across country to be nearer to some loving friends.

On my last day before I moved I decided to go to the beach and meditate for a while in the hopes of finally closing the door on that era, so I could move on. As I sat there looking out at the sparkling water a vision began to form.

Now the "pros" would probably say it was the hallucination of a hysterical woman, or the workings of an over active imagination—I don't care. What I saw was my dead love hovering out there above the water. In the moment he appeared, I burst into racking sobs. The grief was just as intense as it was the moment I learned of his death. I was incredulous and despondent. How could it be that after all the processing I had done, I would be feeling this deep unbearable grief—still?

I looked at him through my tears and I thought to myself "is this hideous grief going to be with me the rest of my life--the rest of eternity?" He actually nodded his head yes! I thought "you mean this is it--the condition of my life forever?" Again he nodded yes. Now I'm thinking, "How can this be? How can I do this?" and then I realized or understood or heard him say that I had to accept this into my universe before I could move on. That was the last piece, the only thing I had not done. I had not accepted it or embraced it or owned it as mine, as me. I had been trying to make the grief go away instead of embracing it and taking it into my being.

Sitting there on the sand I decided to create a place for him in my space. I imagined an ornate chair for him to sit in and placed it beside me and invited him to sit there. To this day I can put my attention on that chair and go right to the incredible memories we shared and the grief I experienced when all that was taken away.

I learned that by integration, and only by integration, can an experience be completed and no longer experienced. The only way for me to get on with my life without him was to install my entire experience of him in my universe, give it a place to exist in my awareness, forever. The grieving wasn't about to stop until I did.

What incredible peace this encounter with him brought to my life. When he was still alive he used to say "we have work to do together." I sometimes wonder if that understanding that came to me on the beach that day was the work he referred to.

Learning #6: Separation precipitates experience. Integration creates completion and experience ceases.

Chapter Four Main Points:

We really do choose what we are experiencing. Learning to be in control of those choices is what empowers a deliberate, happy, relaxed, and peaceful life.

Learning #6: Separation precipitates experience. Integration creates completion and experience ceases.

5

The Experiencer

"People have believed they are human beings seeking a spiritual experience. When in actuality, they are spiritual beings immersed in the human experience."

Wayne Dyer (quoting de Chardin). Wayne Dyer, born 1940, is an internationally renowned author and speaker in the field of self-development. De Chardin, a visionary French Jesuit, paleontologist, biologist, and philosopher, who spent the bulk of his life trying to integrate religious experience with natural science, most specifically Christian theology with theories of evolution. 1881-1955

If I want to experience being a woman/man, parent/child, lover, friend, etc., I must separate enough to experience that other person as separate from myself, thus an identity is created with which to have a particular experience. Identities are simply collections of thoughts, ideas, desires, resistances, memories, indoctrinations, etc. that collectively make up the vehicles which enable us to have experiences. I notice that when I'm in the company of my mother I automatically adopt the identity of daughter. That identity is made up of our entire histories together. When I'm with my children I adopt the identity of mom and so it goes.

There are degrees of resistance and desire in our lives which determine whether we enjoy ourselves or not. We could put the various levels of experiencing on a scale with extreme resistance on one end of the scale and extreme desire on the other end. If you put a zero in the middle and extend numbers from one to a hundred out in either direction then

extreme resistance would be a hundred on one end and extreme desire*
would be a hundred at the other end. Those high numbers are the things
that I try to keep under control by integrating them as quickly as I can
identify them. The most subtle form of resistance is to say Not Me. The
purest form of integration is Me.

*Desire is simply the resistance to not having something. It really
does come down to two things: not resisting and resisting, Me and
Not Me.

Now let's revisit the story about Mark, the guy with the shoulder
pain. Had I had the tools then that I have now, I would probably have
suggested that he integrate the identity of the son being abused by
his father. That would have handled not only the shoulder pain but
a whole host of other issues that probably existed in his life regarding
that relationship. This process of integrating identities handles issues so
quickly and so thoroughly, it is remarkable.

Integration is like being merged. In order for me to experience ease
with some of my life experiences, I must create a place for them to exist
seamlessly within my universe and simply not be in resistance to their
existence.

Learning #7: Identities come and identities go and none of them are
who I am. They are created constructs designed to allow me to have
experiences. Who I am is the creator, originator of those identities, and
I can play in them or not – I decide.

Therefore Me, the authentic me, would be the spiritual being having
a human experience. Not Me would be all those created constructs
put into place in order for Me to have that human experience. To be
able to become who we want to be is a matter of integrating enough of
those created constructs for us to get back to the experience of our own
divinity, to return to our natural state of peace and happiness.

Chapter Five Main Points:

Learning #7: Identities come and identities go and none of them are who I am. They are created constructs designed to allow me to have experiences. Who I am is the creator, originator of those identities, and I can play in them or not – I decide.

Just about everything can be demonstrated on a scale. The intensity of an experience can be determined by its position on a scale. zero at the center being Me and the not Me experiencing identity located anywhere on that scale extending out towards degrees of desire or resistance.

Desire < 75_50_25_0_25_50_75 > resistance

< < < < < < not Me < < < < **Me** > > > > not Me > > > > > >

On this scale Me exists at the center at zero. Not Me exists in various degrees extending out from that center towards either end of the scale.

6

Mind Body - Body Mind

The Bhagavad-Gita declares that there are no outward signs of enlightenment.

The Bhagavad-Gita ~ Sanskrit: Song of God, also known as the Gita—written 3000 BC, it is considered among the most important texts in the history of literature and philosophy.

There is a saying: "What we focus on expands." Given the understandings I had come to regarding attention and experiences, that was easy to see, but where does it expand? Do these things we focus on expand in the physical universe, or just in our minds?

The reason I asked that question is I had seen people running around for years declaring their prosperity and they weren't any better off financially than when they started.

In meditation practice we were taught to clear our minds of all thought, to quiet the monkey mind*. This is a wonderful skill and it has many applications from calming physical symptoms to giving us a more peaceful and expanded outlook on life.

A friend who was helping me edit this book found this exercise so valuable she wanted me to include it. It happens to be one of my all time favorites so I agreed and here it is:

---

* Monkey Mind - that aspect of consciousness which generates thoughts that seem out of our deliberation or control.

An Exercise to Quiet the Monkey Mind

Find a quiet place where you can relax without distractions.

Step 1 – Deliberately focus your attention on something in the room other than yourself. Study that thing intently; observe it until your attention is fully on it. Take your time.

Step 2 – Now bring your attention back onto yourself. Observe everything you are experiencing. Your body temperature, any sensations you may be having, you may be able to hear your own heartbeat, and include any thoughts you may be having.

Step 3 – Continue moving your attention between things outside yourself and then back to yourself. Do this until you can accomplish the shift of attention quite easily. Be patient—this could take a while.

Step 4 – When you are certain you have the ability to fully place your attention where you want it, then place your attention on your mind, and say these words: "Go ahead mind, say anything you want, you have all of my attention."

What happens is nearly magical. Your mind stops in its tracks! Quiet—no sound— nothing but serene peace is left.

If your mind chatter doesn't stop, go back to step one and continue alternating your attention between objects outside yourself and yourself until your skill strengthens before continuing to step four. The outcome of mastering this skill is absolutely worth the effort required to accomplish it. A quiet mind—who knew it could be this easy?

However, I never did make anything manifest in the physical domain through meditation alone. Like everything else I learned over the years, every question can have many answers. Solutions frequently have more than one component.

A Story about the Guy in the Attic

Many years ago I found myself living in a huge house all by myself and minus one annoying husband. Since I was very much into the exploration of everything metaphysical I decided to turn that house into an intentional community*. What a great time that was! The tolerance for each others' endeavors was pretty much unlimited as long as they were not dangerous or detrimental to the community.

*Intentional community--an environment capable of supporting a variety of individuals with common interests working together to support each other's explorations.

There was a guy who was a part of the household who was determined to create the relationship of his dreams, his ideal mate. This guy sat in the attic and wrote affirmations for one solid year in the attempt to *create* this partner. He would talk about her at meals as though he had already met her. He did visualizations about her, he meditated on her, and he even said that he could feel her presence sometimes.

None of us ever met her because the only place she existed was in his mind! She was real there; he was experiencing her there, but she didn't appear in the physical universe because he had not taken any action to create her there.

One day I asked him if he had considered going out into the world to meet this person. Would he consider perhaps going to a meeting or to a church or anyplace where humans gather? One other day I asked him if he thought she was going to drop down the chimney like Santa Claus. He said I had offended him and he moved out of the attic. The last I heard he was still single.

Learning #8: Unless I change something, nothing is going to change. If I create something in my mind, it will only manifest in my mind. If

I want it to manifest in the physical, I have to do something physical. Body-Mind, these are two parts of a whole thing.

Chapter Six Main Points:

Embracing a resisted experience and giving it a place to exist within our awareness can seem to be the opposite of what we need to do in order to cease the experience of something and that is why we have not been successful in that before.

The realization of what integration really is and how powerful it is was the conception of the birth of the Me, not Me technique and this book. The absolute acceptance and merging with things we consider not Me is so simple it seemed incredulous to me. And, at the end of the day, it simply works.

Learning #8: Unless I change something, nothing is going to change. If I create something in my mind, it will only manifest in my mind. If I want it to manifest in the physical, I have to do something physical. Body-Mind, these are two parts of a whole thing.

7

One More Serving Please

"Named must your fear be before banish it you can."
Yoda - a mystical character of Star Wars (movies) fame. He was one of the most renowned Jedi Masters in Galactic history, known for his legendary wisdom, mastery of the force, and skills in light saber combat. Yoda was first introduced to the world by George Lucas in 1980.

Our experience of life as human beings is affected by everything we're exposed to, those things we consider good as well as the bad. We most likely already know what we do or do not like in many areas of our lives. The ability to control or change our resisted experiences is what gives us the ease or calm center from which to enjoy a happier life.

The following is a simple effective exercise with which you will be able to develop a valuable skill. This skill enables you to maximize the benefits you will derive from applying the Me-not Me process to your life.

Also, in order to be self-determined in regards to our experiences, we must be able to be separate from them in order to examine the incident. This will enable us to make a place for them in our universe.

The level of deliberateness we achieve is the direct result of being able to control the focus of our attention on any given subject or experience.

As with all things in our lives we are already able to control our attention toward some of what we experience. There are aspects of each of our lives that we have more or less control over. Practicing all the exercises in this booklet improves the skills we need to gain greater control.

Attention Exercise 3: (Please consider reading all the way through the instructions for this exercise before doing it.)

Put your attention on some experience you didn't like or that was upsetting to you. Notice how you feel. Notice if you feel any tightness in your body or emotional upset. Now allow yourself to have that experience just as it is, without resisting it or attempting to make it go away. Continue to notice if your physical sensations escalate. Now imagine that you are sitting in a theater watching that experience as though it is a movie. You are now observing it instead of being in the experience of it. Continue observing it for a few seconds. Go back and forth between being actively involved in the experience and then watching it. You are shifting between being an experiencer and an observer. Continue doing this until you feel comfortable doing it. Notice if the exerience begins to affect you less physically. It's ok whether it does or not; just notice.

Now relax and bring your attention back to yourself.

Next, choose an experience that was pleasant for you. Notice how it makes you feel. Notice if you feel physical pleasure. Allow yourself to have that experience just as it is. Don't try to change it or hold on to it. Continue to notice if your physical sensations escalate. Now imagine that you are sitting in a theater watching that experience as though it is a movie. Observe it for a few seconds. Go back and forth between being actively involved in the experience and then watching it. You are shifting between being an experiencer and being an observer. Continue doing this until you feel comfortable doing it. Notice if the experience begins to effect you less physically. It's ok whether it does or not, just notice.

Now relax and bring your awareness back to yourself.

Continue doing this exercise until you feel that you have acquired the skill of shifting between being involved in an experience and watching it like a movie.

There are things you want to make "Me" (integrate) and things you want to make or keep as "Not Me" (continue to experience). The ability to determine/decide what is ME and what is NOT ME is what we have been in training for with the exercises we have done previously.

Learning #9: I get to decide what my life is going to be like, not anyone or anything outside of me, just me!

Chapter Seven Main Points:

Everything counts. From learning to name the experiences we have to increasing our ability to focus on them all improve our internal locus of control and improve our chances of having the lives we prefer.

Learning #9: I get to decide what my life is going to be like, not anyone or anything outside of me, just me!

8

The Me, not Me Technique:
Seven Steps to Freedom

"The first rule is to keep an untroubled spirit.
The second is to look things in the face and know them for what
they are."
Marcus Aurelius ~ (April 121 to March 180) was the emperor of Rome
from 161 to 180. He was the last of the "Five Good Emperors" and is
considered one of the most stoic philosophers. His work *Meditations*
written in Greek is still revered as a literary monument to a philosophy
of service and duty.

As you move into the Me, not Me technique please read it through
to familiarize yourself, and become comfortable, with each step before
applying it to your experiences.

1 - Look at your life and identify what you want to change. What
are you experiencing you do not prefer?

This step is most powerful when you are actively involved in some
undesired experience. I don't recommend making lists of things to process.
Simply use the Me, not Me Process to handle things as they occur.

2 - Allow yourself to feel all the sensations associated with that
experience. Be involved with it. Notice any identity* (or part*
of yourself) that presents itself as having that experience. Put
your attention on the identity having those sensations-- have

the experience as that identity (or part) for a few minutes until you feel that you are there.

Identity--this could be you as a child or you at any other point in your life. It will be a representation of you during this lifetime (or any other lifetime) having this experience. However it shows up just let it be ok.

Another way we have of referring to our identities is calling them parts of us. I.e. "Part of me wants to stop grieving but another part of me isn't sure it's possible." That "part" of you is the identity I'm referring to. Whether you experience this identity as a defined persona or simply a part of yourself—either is fine and will work perfectly with this process.

Observe it for a few minutes—watch it like a movie—until you can see that "that" is an identity (not you). Go back and forth between existing as it and watching it a few times.

As described earlier, use the movie theatre example to create the experience of being the identity (or part of yourself) and then not being it. Have your self (Me) sitting in the audience of the theatre and the identity(the not Me) up on the movie screen acting out the experience. Notice the identities behavior, language, interactions with others, and posture. Be aware that you are in the audience watching the identity acting out the experience. When you feel at ease with moving between the movie screen as experiencer and being in the audience as observer then go on to the next step.

3 - Locate a place* in your field of awareness where that identity would feel safe, welcome, and comfortable enough to stay forever. Make this a place where you can leave the identity without having to hold it or maintain attention on it. Invite the identity to join you there if it isn't already there.

You could visualize a place in a park, beside a stream or under a tree. It could be in a building that you mentally construct just for this occasion.

It could be a place that you are familiar with or one that you just imagine on the spot. Just as long as the "identity" feels safe, welcome and comfortable there it will work.

4 - Be there with the identity. Have a conversation with it. If it has things it wants to say, let it. If it has questions, answer them. Stay there until the identity feels relaxed and complete. If you have things you want to say to it or questions you want to ask it, go ahead. This is a completion for "both" of you. Take whatever time you need to become relaxed and quiet—until you feel like there is nothing else to say or do.

Give this step plenty of time. No need to rush. Then when you both feel complete go on to step 5.

5 - Say out loud "I love you. I thank you for all you've done for me. You will always be part of Me." Or you can use your own phrasing; just include the ideas expressed here.

The idea here is unconditional acceptance into the totality of your universe. If you hit resistance with any of the steps of this process simply go back to the previous step and stay with it until you feel comfortable enough to continue.

6 - After you both feel quiet, relaxed and complete then say out loud "I'm going to go do something else now."

Simply get up and walk away leaving no attention on the identity or its' experience.

7 - Allow some time to adjust to this integration. You may want to go for a walk, or have a cup of tea, whatever you'd like to do. Then refocus your attention and energy to making some decisions about what you would like to experience next.

Remember, we choose what we experience. Make some choices about experiences you desire to have now.

This will become a very fast and organic process. You will quickly learn to recognize those things you wish to integrate and move right into this process. The more you do this process the more you will experience yourself as the "Me" that we all are, complete and whole. Remember, we are here to have a human experience. Now you get to choose what your life will be.

Chapter Eight Main Points:

1 - Look at your life and identify what you want to change. What are you experiencing you do not prefer

2 - Allow yourself to feel all the sensations associated with that experience. Be involved with it. Notice any identity* (or part* of yourself) that presents itself as having that experience. Put your attention on the identity having those sensations-- have the experience as that identity (or part) for a few minutes until you feel that you are there.

3 - Locate a place* in your field of awareness where that identity would feel safe, welcome, and comfortable enough to stay forever. Make this a place where you can leave the identity without having to hold it or maintain attention on it. Invite the identity to join you there if it isn't already there.

4 - Be there with the identity. Have a conversation with it. If it has things it wants to say, let it. If it has questions, answer them. Stay there until the identity feels relaxed and complete. If you have things you want to say to it or questions you want to ask it, go ahead. This is a completion for "both" of you. Take whatever time you need to become relaxed and quiet—until you feel like there is nothing else to say or do.

5 - Say out loud "I love you. I thank you for all you've done for me. You will always be part of Me." Or you can use your own phrasing; just include the ideas expressed here.

6 - After you both feel quiet, relaxed and complete then say out loud "I'm going to go do something else now."

7 - Allow some time to adjust to this integration. You may want to go for a walk, or have a cup of tea, whatever you'd like to do. Then refocus your attention and energy to making some decisions about what you would like to experience next and leaves, walk away.

9

That Was Then This Is Now!

"I have integrated all my creations."
~ Howard Wayne Goss, dear friend. 1934 - 1996

I was explaining to a friend that a way of managing my life is the use of what I refer to as "policies." Sometimes in life a situation would present to me that needed some heavy handed management in order to keep me out of trouble. A policy is a rule that I would establish to effect that management. These rules are not negotiable, never ignored, and serve to protect me from falling prey to the challenges inherent in participating in our present day civilization. I would assess the dangerous or undesirable situation, come up with a solution that would prevent me from endangering myself in such a situation, and then author a policy to handle it. I didn't create a lot of these policies. I didn't want to burden my life with too many rules to keep track of. In the end I established four policies.

If someone I'm involved with or I'm relating to objects to my policies, that's okay. I just look elsewhere for companionship.

A little back story might help with the explanation of my creation of policies. In the early 80s the AIDS virus was ravaging this U.S. I had a number of friends fall victim to the disease and die pretty ugly deaths as a result. I have a number of friends who are still dealing with HIV and they have been in various levels of treatment all these years. The loss of the ones who didn't survive was heartbreaking. Watching these once outrageously alive vibrant beings reduced to wasted, near corpses affected me so deeply I vowed to do whatever it took to prevent myself or anyone I knew from this fate.

One of the first policies I established was this: I would not ever engage in a sexual encounter with any person without first both of us having a full panel of STD testing at a clinic licensed for this purpose. Further, we would exchange documents to verify the testing and make agreements regarding the exclusive nature of our physical relationship. They also had to agree to employ safe sex practices. If either or both of us decided to end the exclusivity clause then we could still be friends but I would no longer engage in sexual activity with them.

In addition to this policy I take every opportunity to educate my friends, clients, and even acquaintances in the use of condoms, complete with a long list of what I hope are compelling arguments in favor of their use. I've even made myself the local expert on the use of female condoms. I keep a supply of both kinds on hand at all times, even when I'm traveling, to offer to anyone in need of one.

Any time someone objects to my policy, the first image that springs to mind is the vision of my darling friends' body melting away as he died of this heinous disease and my resolve is instantly restored

With this mission in place, I've heard the most astonishing array of excuses for not following this policy. If the best I can do is give out the information and supplies then I've done the best I can do and adhered to my policy. I've always known that people are going to do whatever they are going to do no matter how dire the consequences of irresponsible behaviors. I'm not going to get on a soapbox here. I am however going to add that this policy has served me wonderfully to this day.

I have not contracted any sort of STD in all the years I've been a sexually active person and I intend to keep it that way.

Another policy that I established many years ago is about money. It is about borrowing and lending money. I observed so many times that people who owe me money tend to disappear from my life. Sometimes they would vilify me before leaving in order to justify their departure! I also noticed that if I had borrowed money from someone I would be obsessed with getting it paid back. This obsession would impede my life to an alarming degree. It was clearly time for another policy. My policy regarding borrowing and lending money is this: I won't do it. If a friend is in need and I have the funds available, I will give them the money with no strings attached. If I can't give them all they need I will help them find it. If I need money, and I definitely have in the past, I will ask friends to gift me with whatever portion of my need they can afford to give me. This way I've kept my friends and we've actually become closer in the experience of mutual support.

What do these things have to do with "That was then, this is now" you might ask?

I recently realized, that at the time I established those policies, that was the best method I had of protecting myself from unwise and possibly dangerous decisions made on the spur of the moment or in the heat of passion. At that time I didn't have a reliable way of integrating resisted experiences.

Today, when I encounter a resistance, I use the Me, not Me process to integrate the resistance. I do this so as to not attract those things to me. Remember the section of this book on the experiencer in chapter 5? The lesson being: "what we resist persists and that resistance can actually cause us to attract it." Having to adhere to such rigid policies has not only protected me but has also been a great limitation to my free attention. Now that I know how to integrate resisted experiences, I no longer feel the limitations of those policies.

This is absolutely not to say that I have thrown caution to the wind regarding safe sex or abandoned the policies I so carefully constructed.

I still very much follow the guidelines of my policies and that includes all the components of the original policies. The difference now is that rather than operating from fear and resistance, I am now clearly choosing to behave in this way. As a result I don't attract individuals who try to tempt me to do otherwise.

It's been an interesting shift in my consciousness. I've changed from being driven by fear to deliberately choosing. I now feel more powerful and deliberate in the choices I make. Divesting myself of fearful motivations and resisted experiences is equal to freedom for me.

Creating policies from fear and resistance – that was then. Creating experiences from choice – this is now. Welcome to a future of peace and ease.

Acknowledgments

"Don't die with your music still in you."
Wayne Dyer ~ Wayne Dyer, born 1940, is an internationally renowned author and speaker in the field of self-development. I consider him to be one of the greatest teachers of compassion of our time.

This work, and the technique that was developed out of it, is a distillation of all the courses, techniques, books, and practices that I have studied in my life, all the teachers I've sat in front of and the stories of all the people who have so generously shared their experiences with me. I have always been humbled by the willingness of the people who have walked through my life to be so vulnerable and to share themselves with me. If I have anything to offer today it is because of all of you. My gratitude for you knows no bounds and I love each and every one of you with an eternal and burning passion.

Of special note are some amazing beings who have not only been an inspiration to me with their demonstrations of determination to improve their own lives but also with their loyalty to our quest—and their single minded insistence that I write this stuff down.

Dawn Nissen came to me, many years ago, when I was at the pinnacle of the traveling era of my career. She walked into my life and seamlessly took over all the aspects of my business that I simply didn't have time to cover. The level of integrity she operates in is an inspiration to all who know her. Dawn made my life a whole lot more of what I wanted it to be. Working together as closely as we did, we became fast friends and to this day she is one of the few beings who never forgets who I really am. When I need it she gently reminds me. Her patience with me is astonishing and her determination that I get this written has been unwavering. Without her this book would certainly have not ever happened.

Ellen Hope is one of those rare beings who demonstrates qualities of loyalty and support unparalleled in my experience. During a recent bout with an illness that took me to Germany for treatment Ellen was on Skype with me every day twice a day for 100 consecutive days without fail. She was constantly vigilant about my condition and my needs. Ellen was always searching her data bank to come up with suggestions supporting my healing and easing my discomfort. This display of compassion and caring is the expression of the essence that I have always experienced with her. For obvious reasons she has been one of my "go to" persons for years. In addition to her assistance in the development of the Me, not Me process Ellen has been constant in her encouragement to finish this project.

In addition to Dawn and Ellen there is a community of dedicated, supportive beings who, in addition to being determined to keep me alive, have relentlessly insisted that I get my work written down. I also want to thank Mark and Carol Jaeger who have been understanding and loving companions since the earliest days of my explorations. I met Katie Purvis during a transition time in my life and she has been an insightful and loyal companion in our deepest, and often hilarious, explorations of life options. When things turned "serious" with the onset of an illness she was not only instrumental in getting me to Germany for treatment, she single handedly nursed me back to health after my return from Europe. Stella Newman came into my life through one of those special connections that happen if we're paying attention and has consistently brought balance, humor and wisdom to our observations of life. Stella has been the bright spot in my day more often than she realizes. Ken Stammer and Valwe LaFosse came through like magicians when I needed them the most. Michelle Hatfield has been totally present with all manner of support and loving encouragement ever since we first met and especially during my journey to recovery. Linda Decker has been a light hearted buddy, teacher, student, and invaluable copy editor.

Without the unwavering support and physical assistance of Young Grey I would have surely not made it through the illness I dealt with for 12 years. As were Paul Elison and Linda Rust, Joanie Babcock, Bob and Dani Short, Sharon and Peter Kafoed and Keats Elliot who without hesitation got me to Germany for life saving medical treatments. Also Shauna VanDerHoek, Joanne Reeves, Darlene Funk and Holly Riley who take turns with me being each others mother and daughter. My dearest Harry and Mary Holman, my son Andy and, in his own special way, my friend Max.

These loving beings are demonstrations of the best that humans can aspire to 'show up as' in the world. They have shared their lives, their families and their processes with me without reservation and without fail. They have been there for me in countless ways and have allowed me to learn by being there for them. They have helped me develop the techniques taught in this process and they have helped me write it all down. They are truly the family of my heart.

Without the rich storehouse of life experiences provided by my natal family, my life would surely have been vectored into a different and probably less interesting path.

I could fill an entire book with the names of all those beautiful beings who have supported, shared, taught, studied, traveled, laughed, cried, survived, processed, explored, and died with me. In short, this list includes all those amazing people who have shared the cornucopia of human experiences with me. You all know who you are and hopefully just how precious you are to me and how grateful I am for you. When I count my blessings I count each of you twice.

Epilogue

*"Extraordinary opportunities come your way when
you seek to connect with others for mutual gain, for
the sheer joy of it and for the good of the planet."*
Gil Ortega - Lead generation expert. He is a fellow traveler through
cyber adventures and a ray of hope when inspiration seemed scarce.

I have published this book without including the usual limitations
to the readers regarding the use and sharing of the information for
several reasons.

First, I didn't want to spend the rest of my precious life monitoring
the distribution of something that has been created as a result of the
collected and assimilated works of so many brilliant teachers who came
before me. Take it, it's yours. Apply it, share it, and teach it if you feel
qualified to do so. I hope you will at least entertain this as the possibility
it is, and above all, I hope you will enjoy it.

My next reason is that I have been sifting through personal
development and self help stuff for decades. I've come to some
conclusions, had some "learnings" and I didn't want to leave this human
experience without having shared them. In all my years of exploring
consciousness I haven't found anything, that falls outside of the concepts
discussed here, that is any more powerful or any more revealing than
this. If I had I would have included it.

Last but certainly not least, I suspect that my grandchildren perceive me as a bit odd. I certainly show up in the world differently than other adults they encounter. For that reason I hope that one day they will read this and grasp an understanding of why that was so and maybe even consider using this tool to enhance the quality of their own lives!

Now, go create the life you really want! Never settle for less.

"I would rather have thirty minutes of wonderful than a lifetime of nothing special."
Julia Roberts ~ in the movie *Steel Magnolias*

One last note: I did my best to write this book in plain English. I have deliberately not used a lot of new age jargon. When I found it necessary to use a word not in common usage I attempted to define it as accurately as possible. I didn't want this book to be about you developing another vocabulary. My intention is for you to use the information to have a new life!

Resources

"It would be so nice if something would make sense for a change."
Alice from Alice's Adventures in Wonderland written by Charles Lutwidge Dodgson (under the pseudonym Lewis Carroll) in 1865

If you would like to explore some of the background of these materials or if you would like some support in applying this process to your life, then I suggest you connect one of the coaches who are most qualified in the application of this technique.

Please read the "Meet the Coaches" section at the end of this book to discover the individual qualifications of each of the coaches.

Talley HO!
Kayt Campbell

Book Recommendation: *Allowing* by Holly Riley—A Portrait of Forgiving and Letting Life Love You.
www.hollyriley.com

Announcing the completion of Kayt's latest book
The Ultimate Speed Dating Secret – The 5 Minute Interview

Do you seem to be picking all the wrong people to date? Have you searched the world and still not found your person? Do you feel like you're stumbling around in the dark looking for a needle in a haystack?

The technique I teach in The Ultimate Speed Dating Secret - The 5 Minute Interview took 20 years to perfect and has been taught to hundreds of clients all over the world. They've used it with so much success that they begged me to "put it out into the world". So I am. Here it is. The information and method of cutting right to the chase in one simple-to-learn conversation can turn your first meeting into a discovery process that will change your thinking about dating forever.

The Ultimate Speed Dating Secret – The 5 Minute Interview

"Kayt, this is so simple and makes so much sense . . . I can't believe I didn't think of it myself. But I'm glad you did and that you taught it to me. Thanks mate!" ~ C.L. New South Wales, NZ

Would you like to have some guidance with the use of the Me, not Me process? Check out this special offer!

Each Coach offers a 50% discount for an introductory coaching session. This session will include an evaluation of your needs and desires, an explanation of our services and actual work with the process taught in the book *Me, not Me—Becoming Who You Want To Be By Recovering From Your Past*. When you email the coach of your choice she will connect with you, either via Email or by telephone--your choice, to determine the best time and date for your session. Enjoy the journey!

Kayt Campbell kayt.campbell.mnmcoach@gmail.com

Dawn Nissen dawn.nissen.mnmcaoch@gmail.com

EllenHope ellen.hope.mnmcoach@gmail.com

We are ready to answer questions you may have about our coaching services and to serve your coaching needs. Be sure to check the website frequently for future offers

~ MeNotMebook.com

MEET THE COACHES

The Author-My name is Kayt Campbell and I live in San Diego, California. The focus of my life and career has been the acquisition and mastery of self help (life improvement) technologies. The friends I have made along the way and the clients I have worked with are the most exciting people I know. Anyone who wants to not only improve the quality of their lives but also go for their dreams is of primary interest to me.

TESTIMONIAL: When I first started coaching with Kayt I was in a lot of pain with a re-occurring health issue. Kayt, has a wide range of coaching tools that we used very successfully. In a short amount of time I was out of pain and was going to end our coaching sessions. I was encouraged to not settle for just being pain free but to go for MY DREAMS! I am so glad that I continued as I am the happiest I have ever been in my life. I keep up leveling my life and today my health, wealth, relationships and outlook on life are incredible. I am also a life coach and I highly recommend Kayt to any person who wants to create a magnificent life with truly lasting results. B.E., CA

Kayt Campbell has spent her life teaching the principles in this book to people all over the world. She is an expert at motivating and training people to pursue their best lives. If you would like her to customize a personal appearance for your team or organization she can be contacted at <u>kayt.campbell.MnMcoach@gmail.com</u>

COACH: My name is Dawn Nissen and I have been a student of human behavior all my life. Being a wife, mother, entrepreneur, businesswoman and teacher gave me ample opportunities to do this. I began studying self-improvement techniques, in my early adult life, by reading and listening to courses on tape and eventually attending seminars. This was primarily to find a way to do my life without so much struggle. Through these studies I have gathered the knowledge and experience I needed in order to have the life I wanted. This pursuit has brought me to the ability to offer guidance as people work through confusing or difficult life lessons. Assisting others to learn and grow in knowledge and confidence and develop the clarity to be in charge of their life is one of the most rewarding things I do.

TESTIMONIAL: Dawn is one of the best life coaches, her ability to listen and guide people through difficult situations is amazing! When I am overwhelmed with worry, Dawn has always been able to remain calm, clear and focused while leading me towards finding the answer. Her compassion is without measure and her intellect a blessing. B.N., TX Dawn can be contacted at: dawn.nissen.MnMcoach@gmail.com

COACH: My name is Ellen hope. Having had a difficult childhood and early adulthood, I have had so many varied and unusual life experiences that my life has enabled me to have a unique understanding and compassion for others and what they have done or experienced in their lives. From a young age I searched for ways to heal myself, to integrate my life experiences and find peace and happiness. My life is committed to evolving. I have 25 years of experience in coaching people plus writing, facilitating and teaching workshops and courses. My passion is empowering others and assisting them in healing, integrating, empowering their lives, and manifesting their dreams

TESTIMONIAL: Ellen has the ability to coach you to a result that exceeds your expectations. When Ellen coached me she had skills to navigate me to hidden places that were responsible for making me feel the way I felt. It happened very fast and very easy and the change was for all time to come. I recommend Ellen to Everyone. She is an amazing life coach and the most loving person to work with. All I felt was safety and willingness to explore with her. M.C.

Ellen can be contacted at: ellen.hope.MnMcoach@gmail.com

And remember to check out Kayt's second book

The Ultimate Speed Dating Secret – The 5 Minute Interview

Printed in the United States
By Bookmasters